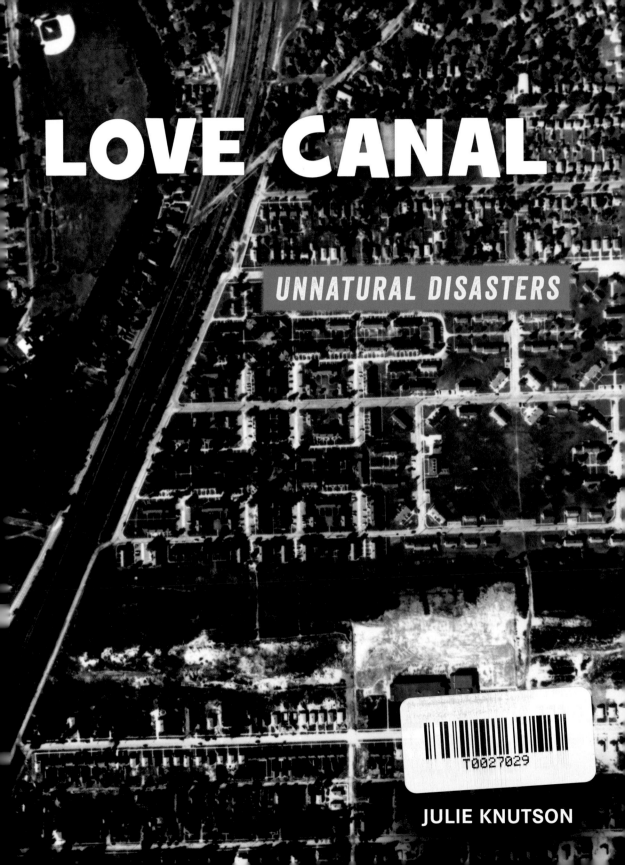

LOVE CANAL

UNNATURAL DISASTERS

T0027029

JULIE KNUTSON

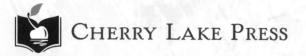

CHERRY LAKE PRESS

Published in the United States of America by Cherry Lake Publishing Group
Ann Arbor, Michigan
www.cherrylakepublishing.com

Reading Adviser: Marla Conn, MS, Ed., Literacy specialist, Read-Ability, Inc.
Photo Credits: © Everett Collection/Shutterstock, cover, 1; © Library of Congress/Published by Detroit
    Publishing Co./Reproduction No.: LC-USZC4-6887, 5; © pnita sintusontichart/Shutterstock, 6; © Library
    of Congress/Published by Detroit Publishing Co./Reproduction No.: LC-DIG-det-4a18780, 9; © Mykola59/
    Shutterstock, 12; © EPA/Love Canal Area Pre-1978, 15; © EPA/Wikimedia, 16; © USGS/The National Map/
    Wikimedia, 19; © EPA/Love Canal Area Evacuated Homes, 20; © CHEJ, 22, 26; © EPA/Love Canal Pre 1982
    Ring 1 Homes, 25

Cherry Lake Press is an imprint of Cherry Lake Publishing Group.

Names: Knutson, Julie, author.
Title: Love Canal / Julie Knutson.
Description: Ann Arbor, Michigan : Cherry Lake Publishing, 2021. | Series: Unnatural disasters : human
    error, design flaws, and bad decisions | Includes index. | Audience: Grades 4-6 | Summary: "Human
    modification of the environment always carries a risk of accident and folly. Explore the causes and
    consequences of the Love Canal disaster of the 1970s in Niagara Falls, New York. Guided by compelling
    questions such as, "What led to this disaster?," "Who was impacted by it?," and "What changed in its
    aftermath?" the interdisciplinary content blends social studies and science. Ultimately, it pushes
    students to consider how humans can meet their need for resources in a safe, sustainable way. Books
    include table of contents, index, glossary, author biography, and timeline"—Provided by publisher.
Identifiers: LCCN 2020039975 (print) | LCCN 2020039976 (ebook) | ISBN 9781534180185 (hardcover) |
    ISBN 9781534181892 (paperback) | ISBN 9781534181199 (pdf) | ISBN 9781534182905 (ebook)
Subjects: LCSH: Love Canal Chemical Waste Landfill (Niagara Falls, N.Y.)—Juvenile literature. | Chemical
    plants—Waste disposal—Environmental aspects—New York (State)—Niagara Falls—Juvenile literature. |
    Hazardous waste sites—New York (State)—Niagara Falls—Juvenile literature. | Pollution—New York
    (State)—Niagara Falls—Juvenile literature.
Classification: LCC TD181.N72 N5133 2021 (print) | LCC TD181.N72 (ebook) |
    DDC 363.72/870974799—dc23
LC record available at https://lccn.loc.gov/2020039975
LC ebook record available at https://lccn.loc.gov/2020039976

Cherry Lake Publishing Group would like to acknowledge the work of the Partnership for 21st Century
Learning, a Network of Battelle for Kids. Please visit http://www.battelleforkids.org/networks/p21
for more information.

Printed in the United States of America
Corporate Graphics

ABOUT THE AUTHOR

Julie Knutson is an Illinois-based author. In her spare moments, she enjoys investigating
new places and ideas alongside her husband, son, and border collie.

TABLE OF CONTENTS

INTRODUCTION

It's early August 1978. Young residents of the Love Canal neighborhood in Niagara Falls, New York, aren't pedaling down sunbaked streets on their bikes. They're not splashing at the public pool or dodging the spray of fire hydrants. Instead, a group of kids stand on a corner near their elementary school. In their hands are protest signs. One is painted with the message, "I hate the Love Canal." Another reads, "My house is worth nothing." A 10-year-old boy named Don Huey tells a reporter, "I don't care how far I have to go [for school]. I want to get away from the canal. The school's right on top of the chemicals."

Just days before, the world of these children, their families, and their neighbors had been turned upside down.

The hydroelectric power created by the running water of Niagara Falls made the area appealing to industrial companies.

Experts confirmed what residents long suspected: their homes and school sat on top of a decaying, toxic waste site that was causing them real harm. The chemicals that oozed up from the ground—in basements, backyards, on the playground—caused a range of health problems, from headaches to serious birth defects to cancer.

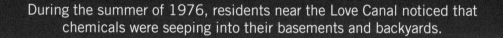

During the summer of 1976, residents near the Love Canal noticed that chemicals were seeping into their basements and backyards.

For too long, city and county officials hadn't listened to their complaints. Now, just days after the president of the United States declared the neighborhood a disaster area, it was time for direct action. All of the neighborhood's residents demanded change.

*President Jimmy Carter declared the Love Canal a disaster area on August 7, 1978. It was the first time in U.S. history that **federal** emergency funds were used for a disaster of a non-natural cause.*

How did more than 20,000 tons of toxins come to lie beneath this 10-block suburb? What effects did these chemicals have on residents? And what tools did citizens use to force action on an issue that the government had ignored for more than two decades?

The Power of the Press and Community Organizing

In the summer of 1978, people beyond the Love Canal neighborhood first learned of the crisis. *Niagara Gazette* reporter Michael H. Brown investigated residents' claims about chemical wastes and toxic sludge. In a series of articles, he exposed the "witch's brew of compounds" that lurked beneath the ground.

While public officials didn't rush to address the problems, residents wanted answers and quick action. Soon, **grassroots** campaigns were launched. Community members banded together to demand the closure of the school, relocation, and financial **compensation**. By August 1978, the national media spotlight fell on these activists fighting for environmental justice.

CHAPTER 1

Before

Nineteenth-century **entrepreneur** William T. Love had a vision. In 1892, Love proposed a "model city" that would harness the awesome power of Niagara Falls to fuel industrial growth. In a business proposal, he called it "one of the greatest undertakings of modern times." To draw manufacturers, the city would offer free electricity for 25 years. The plan also called for giving away free building sites and the construction of 60,000 worker homes. Residents would be lured by the promise of parks, paved streets, and "industrial universities" for training.

Only 1 mile (1.6 kilometers) of the canal was excavated before the project was abandoned.

New York State officials and investors bought into Love's plan. His company began excavating the canal that would connect the "model city" to the **hydroelectric** power source that would serve as its beating heart. On completion, it would boast 500,000 residents. It would be a new kind of city.

But developments in the economy, science, and politics put the brakes on Love's big dream. The financial panic of 1893 scared off investors. Nikola Tesla's discovery of alternating currents shook up the technology world. As Love fought to keep the idea alive, the U.S. government passed legislation to protect Niagara Falls. By 1906, his model city collapsed. All that was left of it was a 1-mile-long (1.6 km) trench, 10 to 40 feet (3 to 12 meters) deep and about 20 yards (18 m) wide.

Over time, the trench returned to nature. Its depths filled with water, and people used it for recreation. For decades after the project was abandoned, Niagarians swam, fished, boated, and skated along this stretch. Eventually, its fate would again change.

Niagara Falls was a manufacturing hub. By 1925, 21 chemical plants operated in the city. About 44 percent of laborers who worked in industry were employed by these companies. Hooker Chemical was the largest chemical company. It had profited from two world wars, producing "50 percent of the synthetic rubber and more than 2.5 billion pounds of chemical products" used during World War II, according to writer Penelope Ploughman.

Niagara Falls' 160-foot (49 m) vertical drop has long captivated visitors. In the late 1800s and early 1900s, many considered the waterfalls to be "the sublimest of nature's works." Today, they continue to draw about 30 million awestruck tourists per year.

Company Towns

Steinway Village, New York. Hershey, Pennsylvania. Pullman, Illinois. The community that William T. Love envisioned was modeled on other company towns that dotted the United States. The idea behind company towns? Draw workers away from big cities with the promise of housing, education, parks, and orderliness.

But these towns weren't **utopias**. Workers couldn't buy their homes. Behaviors were strictly policed. The right to form **unions** was banned. In Pullman, where rail cars were made, **tycoon** George Pullman even chose what books were placed on library shelves and what theater performances were staged. Rather than simply providing a healthy living environment for workers and their families, business owners tried to use these towns to control their labor force. But the strict, **paternal** model often backfired. In 1894, Pullman workers went on strike in Chicago, helping to reset labor relations in the country.

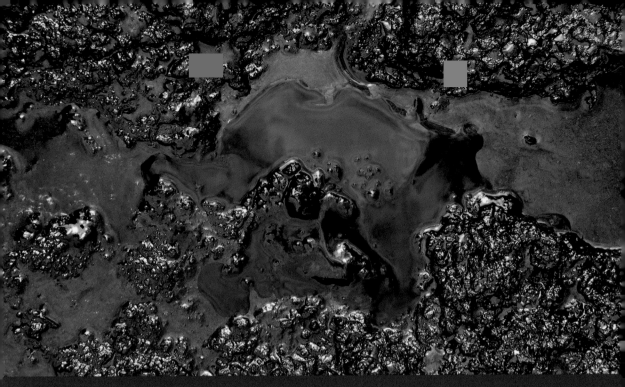

Beginning in the 1940s, the Love Canal was used
as a dump site for toxic chemical waste.

At the same time that Hooker was shipping these products to overseas troops, it was looking for places to dispose of industrial waste. In 1942, the company acquired Love's canal, and for the next 10 years, the 16-acre (6.5 hectares) site functioned as a dumping ground. It was later revealed that Hooker buried 82 different types of chemicals on this land—from pesticides to dyes to materials for making explosives.

[21ST CENTURY SKILLS LIBRARY]

The chemicals were packed in metal drums or fiber containers or sometimes just poured as sludge, gradually filling the canal with toxic trash. In 1952, the site was covered with clay and soil. Grass grew along the canal's **berm**, hiding what lay beneath.

In 1953, Hooker Chemical sold the land to the Niagara Falls School Board for $1. The city needed a new elementary school to meet the needs of a growing population. Ninety-ninth Street Elementary, built atop the filled canal, would meet that demand, welcoming 400 students when it opened in 1955. A whole neighborhood rose up around this school, its homeowners thrilled by brand-new houses and sidewalked streets. They weren't told of the hazards lurking beneath.

*Hooker Chemical disclosed the site's history to the school board. In the documents that sealed the $1 deal, the company noted, "The premises . . . have been filled . . . with waste products resulting from the manufacturing chemicals." Those same documents also **absolved** Hooker of any future risk and liability.*

CHAPTER 2

From "American Dream" to Disaster Zone

Just a few years after moving into their dream homes, some residents of the Love Canal began noticing strange things. For some, sludge seeped through basement walls. It came with foul-smelling fumes that wafted through the entire house. In 1958, three kids suffered chemical burns while playing with "fire rocks" found along the dump. The neighborhood's dogs and cats suffered from patchy fur, skin sores, and shorter-than-expected life spans. Complaints of minor explosions, chemical odors, and open waste were filed by a number of homeowners.

But residents kept on living. Grown-ups tended lawns and gardens. Kids went to school. They played Little League in the summer and built snow forts during the freezing, upstate New York

As the school was being built near the Love Canal, the builders kept hitting soft spots and holes that emitted strong chemical fumes.

winters. It wasn't until the mid-1970s that the community got a major wake-up call about the canal's former life. With record rains and snowfalls, the restless, underground toxins found their way to the surface with greater frequency. On one October morning in 1974, a resident named Karen Schroder looked out her back window to a very surprising sight. With no known cause, the family's pool had been pushed up 2 feet (61 centimeters) out of the ground!

The *Niagara Gazette* was the first news outlet to report the disaster, launching the Love Canal activists.

The next summer, the Schroders set out to replace their pool with a new one made of cement. But after removing the pool, the hole filled with what Karen called "chemical water." These toxic waters flooded the family's yard. They ate away at their wooden fence, which soon collapsed. When the flooding finally receded, the grass and shrubs were scorched and dead.

In 1976, the city of Niagara Falls hired a firm to look into residents' complaints. The company found evidence of chemicals in basements and indoor air. Investigators reported that buried drums were close to breaking through the soil. Traces of toxins were also found in the sewer system. The team offered a plan to **remediate** the issues, but the city didn't act on it.

The Schroders' account and reports from others got the attention of local journalist Michael H. Brown. More record snowfall in 1977 and 1978 led the water table below the ground to swell. When the snow melted, rotted containers ruptured, and their contents bubbled up.

Brown asked the county health department about the issue. Officials dismissed them as a "nuisance." He began interviewing residents and found some alarming patterns. As he later reported in an article in *The Atlantic*, people in the neighborhood were "plagued with ear infections, nervous disorders, rashes, and headaches." Many babies were born with birth defects, including deafness and heart issues.

Brown's findings were first published in the *Niagara Gazette* in April 1978. They captured the attention of Love Canal resident Lois Gibbs, whose children attended Ninety-ninth Street Elementary. Gibbs had no formal community organizing experience. But she was worried. Her son had health problems, and she wondered if they could be connected to the elementary school and the neighborhood. No one else was taking action, so she would. In June 1978, Gibbs formed the Love Canal Parents Movement. Soon, she launched a petition to close the school. As she went door-to-door collecting signatures, she learned that others were fed up too. They were tired of being told, in her words, that they "don't matter."

During a study in 1978, the health department found 81 different chemicals present at the Love Canal site.

Media pressure and early activist efforts forced state officials to finally start testing neighborhood air and soil. Residents were also given blood tests to see if any human health effects could be identified. All through the spring and summer, news about the Love Canal swirled. Evidence that residents were in danger mounted—from high miscarriage rates to steep levels of toxic chemicals like **benzene** in household air.

Only 239 families were relocated in 1978. The remaining 700-plus families near the Love Canal site were deemed as not being at risk despite toxic chemicals present in their homes.

On August 2, 1978, state officials delivered an alarming update. All pregnant women and families with children under age 2 living immediately near the canal were told to leave. Health officials also recommended closing the Ninety-ninth Street School and told residents not to eat food grown in home gardens. Homeowners were terrified and angry. In an effort to protect their rights and ensure access to information, they formed the Love Canal Homeowners Association (LCHA). In the coming years, this group challenged the government to live up to its promise to protect *all* of its citizens.

Less than a week later, the state announced that it would purchase the 239 homes located closest to the canal. But that was less than half of the homes in the 10-block neighborhood. What would happen to the health of those left behind? How could the largely working-class homeowners—whose incomes averaged $10,000 to 25,000 a year—ever be able to recover the value of their properties?

The battle continued. In September, the State Department of Health (DOH) called the Love Canal a "public health time bomb." As work began to remediate the site in the fall and early winter, residents worried about their safety. Protests and marches were held to demand more relocations. Gibbs and her team collected evidence to prove that those outside of the first evacuation "zones" also suffered due to chemical exposure. While the DOH dismissed their findings, news outlets published their compelling data.

Lois Gibbs and other Love Canal activists brought in experts to record evidence of medical harm. They formed a partnership with a researcher at the Roswell Cancer Institute in Buffalo, New York. Among other things, they discovered that babies born to women living in the neighborhood between 1974 and 1978 had a 56 percent chance of having a birth defect.

President Carter and Lois Gibbs at the signing of the bill.
It cost about $17 million to relocate all families from the Love Canal site.

It took more than 2 years of protesting, petitioning, and **lobbying** for all Love Canal residents to win state-supported evacuation. In October and November 1979, families were told to return home after remediation was complete. Many refused. Only after the release of test results on May 17, 1980, that showed widespread **chromosomal** damage across the neighborhood did the Environmental Protection Agency (EPA) recommend that another 710 residents "might" need to be relocated.

[21ST CENTURY SKILLS LIBRARY]

Residents were outraged. The new report showed them to be at increased risk of cancer and reproductive problems. When two EPA representatives came to discuss the report with the LCHA on May 19, they found themselves held hostage in a 5-hour standoff. Gibbs had a message for the White House: relocate all families by Wednesday, May 21, at noon, or else "what we've done here today will look like a Sesame Street picnic."

President Carter finally heard the plea. On Wednesday, May 21, 1980, the White House announced a temporary relocation of the remaining families. And on October 1 of that year, Carter signed a bill **appropriating** federal funds for their permanent rehousing.

The battle for relocation was over. But what was next? What became of this 16-acre (6.5 ha) neighborhood?

Love Canal wasn't the only major environmental disaster of the late 1970s. In March 1979, a partial **meltdown** at the Three Mile Island Nuclear Plant near Harrisburg, Pennsylvania, led to the release of small amounts of radioactive material—and sparked anti-nuclear demonstrations across the United States.

CHAPTER 3

After

It's been more than 40 years since the Love Canal disaster. What's become of the site? What happened to the community leaders who demanded action? How did this disaster change America?

From the early 1980s onward, the EPA worked to contain the Love Canal's waste. The 20,000-plus tons of chemicals were kept in place, rather than dug up and moved. The landfill was first topped with 3 feet (1 m) of clay. A thick sheet of plastic was layered atop it. Finally, 18 inches (46 cm) of topsoil was added as a "seal." Trenches were dug to collect wastewater, and monitoring wells were installed. A carbon filtration system was added to clean up any leaking groundwater.

In 1982, over 200 homes closest to the Love Canal were demolished.

In 1988, the north and west edges of the site were declared "clean." Developers built 200 homes in this formerly evacuated zone, renaming it Black Creek Village. While the EPA insists that regular tests ensure the safety of residents, some who live in the area aren't so sure. In 2011, city workers repairing sewers found pockets of hazardous waste believed to be from the original dump site. And claims in 2013 and 2018 **alleged** that uncontained chemicals continued to do damage.

The Superfund program helps over 40,000 communities
in the United States.

Lois Gibbs wanted to ensure that what happened in Niagara Falls wouldn't happen elsewhere. In 1981, she moved to Virginia and formed the Center for Health, Environment and Justice (CHEJ). Since then, the organization has assisted thousands of other communities battling pollution. In 2003, she was nominated for the Nobel Peace Prize. She is sometimes called the "mother of **Superfund**," a government trust of funds set aside to identify and clean up toxic sites. She has published several books and continues to work for environmental justice.

The Love Canal disaster moved the U.S. environmental movement in new directions. Its activists fought to show that no community should be left sinking in the quicksand of a toxic location. Today, that fight continues, inspired in part by the courageous actions of a group of citizens more than 40 years ago.

Superfund laws were established in 1980, thanks in part to the Love Canal crisis. This federal program run by the EPA provides assistance for cleaning up toxic sites. In June 2019, the EPA listed 1,344 sites as Superfund priorities. They range from old mines in Colorado to decaying chemical plants in Massachusetts. In 2016, it was estimated that 53 million Americans, or 16 percent of the population, lived within 3 miles (5 km) of a Superfund site.

Research & Act

Lois Gibbs led the Love Canal campaign for environmental justice. Soon after, she brought her experience to other communities when she founded CHEJ.

Research Gibbs's life and career. What motivated her to take action? How did she inspire others to join her?

Then, learn more about CHEJ's work today by visiting its website. Focus on recent efforts like the "No Sacrifice Zone!" campaign, which calls out the uneven effects of pollution. As CHEJ notes, "Foul chemicals are not found equally everywhere in our country's air: They are highly concentrated in areas where people have lower incomes and are part of racial minority groups."

Research your city or town. Are there zip codes disproportionately impacted by pollution? What can you do to bring more public attention to this issue? Contact organizations working for change to find out more about how you can help.

Timeline

1942–1952: Hooker Chemical uses the Love Canal for dumping toxic chemicals.

1952: The canal is covered over with soil, burying the toxic waste.

1953: Hooker sells land along the canal to the Niagara Falls School Board for $1; an elementary school will be built on the site.

1976: City of Niagara Falls hires a firm to investigate resident complaints about possible contamination.

1977–1978: Record snow and rainfall in upstate New York cause more buried toxins to surface.

April 1978: *Niagara Gazette* publishes a series of articles on environmental concerns in the neighborhood.

June 1978: Resident Lois Gibbs forms the Love Canal Parents Movement.

August 2, 1978: All pregnant women and families with children under age 2 are ordered to leave the area.

August 7, 1978: President Carter declares the Love Canal a federal disaster.

Fall of 1978–1980: Area residents campaign for widespread relocation; residents are re-housed based on zones.

October 1, 1980: President Carter signs a bill authorizing the relocation of all remaining Love Canal residents.

1981: Lois Gibbs forms the Center for Health, Environment and Justice.

Further Research

"Decision Making: Voices from the Field, Lois Gibbs." *Voices in Leadership*, Harvard University, T.H. Chan School of Public Health, December 23, 2015, www.hsph.harvard.edu/voices/events/gibbs/.

Love Canal. Center for Health, Environment and Justice, depts.washington.edu/envir202/Readings/Reading05.pdf.

Olsen, J.P. *The Love Canal Disaster: Toxic Waste in the Neighborhood* (video). Retro Report, *New York Times*, November 26, 2013, youtu.be/Kjobz14i8kM.

Woods, Michael, and Mary B. Woods. *Environmental Disasters.* Minneapolis, MN: Lerner, 2008.

Glossary

absolved (ab-ZAHLVD) to be cleared of wrongdoing

alleged (uh-LEJD) to say something is true without offering proof

appropriating (uh-PROH-pree-ayt-ing) setting aside funds for a specific need

benzene (BEN-zeen) a harmful chemical found in certain coal and gas products, known to cause cancer

berm (BURM) the upper strip of land that borders a canal

chromosomal (kroh-muh-ZOH-muhl) related to strands that make up the "package" of DNA, which contains genetic information

compensation (kahm-puhn-SAY-shuhn) money given to someone for some loss or injury they have suffered

entrepreneur (ahn-truh-pruh-NUR) a person who organizes, launches, and operates a business

federal (FED-ur-uhl) the central, as opposed to local or state, government

grassroots (GRAS-roots) a movement led by the people, from the ground up

hydroelectric (hye-droh-ih-LEK-trik) electricity generated through the power of water

lobbying (LAH-bee-ing) seeking to influence a public official on an issue

meltdown (MELT-doun) an accident in a nuclear reactor that happens when fuel overheats and melts the surrounding core and equipment

paternal (puh-TUR-nuhl) fatherly

remediate (rih-MEE-dee-ate) to fix or correct

Superfund (SOO-pur-fuhnd) a U.S. federal program set up in 1980 to fund the cleanup of toxic waste

tycoon (tye-KOON) a wealthy, powerful businessperson

unions (YOON-yuhnz) organized associations of workers

utopias (yoo-TOH-pee-uhz) imagined, perfect places

INDEX